Let's Talk About
ACCEPTING "NO"

Written by Joy Berry   Illustrated by Roey

Hello, my name is Rowley.
I'd like to tell you a story
about my friend, T.J.

Like T.J., you might not like it when people tell you, "No."

When someone tells you, "No," you might
- feel frustrated,
- feel angry,
- feel disappointed, and
- feel sorry for yourself.

People are likely to tell you, "No" when you are being unreasonable. You are being unreasonable when you ask for something that is dangerous.
If you do not want to be told, "No," do not ask for anything that could be harmful to anyone or anything.

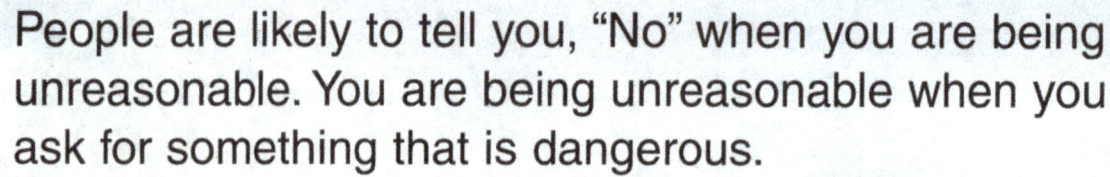

That could be harmful!

You are being unreasonable when you ask for something that is against the rules. If you do not want to be told, "No," do not ask for anything that does not go along with the rules.

You are being unreasonable when you ask for something that is unfair.
If you do not want to be told, "No," do not ask for more than your fair share of something.

What T.J. is requesting is not fair. And anyway, I don't have any cookies.

People are likely to tell you, "No" when you are being inconsiderate. You are being inconsiderate when you care more about yourself than about others.
If you do not want to be told, "No," think about the other person. Make sure that the person has the time and energy to listen and respond to you.

I wonder if I should ask Mom to play with me now?

Only if you want her to say, "No."

You are being inconsiderate when you interrupt others.
If you do not want to be told, "No," do not ask a person for something when he or she is
- involved in a conversation or
- doing something else.

Only if you want him to say, "No."

People are likely to tell you, "No" when you are being impolite.
You are being impolite when you ask for something in an annoying or a bossy way.
If you do not want to be told, "No," be polite. Talk in a courteous way. Try to
- speak calmly and
- avoid being demanding.

If you do not want to be told, "No," be polite.
Use courteous words such as
- "May I please..." or
- "Will you please..."

There are some things that you can do to make yourself feel better when someone tells you, "No."

Remember that every person is told, "No" at one time or another. It is impossible for people to have everything that they request.

People say, "No" to me, too.

Talk to the person who tells you, "No."
Try to find out the reasons for the answer.
Understanding the reasons for the
person's answer might help you to accept it.

Sometimes you might understand the person's reason for saying, "No," but you still might not like the answer.

Discuss your feelings with the person in a kind way. If the person does not give you a different answer, stop asking.

Begging and nagging might result in a decision that is not good for anyone.

You'd better forget the candy!

Accept it when a person says, "No."
Do not whine or throw a tantrum.
Instead, cooperate as much as possible.
The more you cooperate with the person who has told you, "No," the more likely it is that the person will say, "Yes" the next time you make a request.

That sounds fair to me.

Continuing to think about a "No" answer will only frustrate you and make you feel bad.
Try to think about something else.
Try to get involved in doing something else.

You may not like cooperating when someone tells you, "No."
But, it is best for everyone when you do cooperate.

CREDITS

Senior Editor ....Marilyn Berry

Managing Editor ....Keith D. Stewart

Project Manager ....Jim Wools

Print Production Manager ....Joe Cudmore

Copy Editor ....Tom McIntyre

Electronic Production ....Tonia Farnell, Grace Guerra-Milke
Marty Osckel, Dan Dever

Editorial Consultants ....Lisa Berry, Carol Sauder, Mel Sauder

Copyright © Joy Berry, 2022
Originally Published, 1986

All rights are reserved.

No part of this book can be duplicated or used without the prior written permission of the copyright owner, except for the use of brief quotations from the book.

For inquiries or permission requests contact the publisher.

Published by Joy Berry Enterprises
www.joyberryenterprises.com

www.ingramcontent.com/pod-product-compliance
Lightning Source LLC
Chambersburg PA
CBHW081411070526
44583CB00020B/2765